D0772225

TALES OF HORROR
ZOMBIES

by Jim Pipe

BEARPORT
PUBLISHING

New York, New York

Credits

Art Archive: 21; Corbis: 9, 17, 30; Everett/Rex Features: Cover, Title Page, 5; The Kobal Collection: 4, 20–21; Shutterstock: 6, 7, 10–11, 13, 14, 19, 23, 24–25, 30–31; Superstock: 14–15; ticktock Media image archive: 8, 16, 18, 26, 27, 28, 29; Steve Truglia (prostunts.net): 12; Stuart Westmorland/Stone/Getty Images: 8.

Library of Congress Cataloging-in-Publication Data

Pipe, Jim, 1966-
  Zombies / by Jim Pipe.
      p. cm. – (Tales of horror)
  Includes index.
  ISBN-13: 978-1-59716-207-4 (library binding)
  ISBN-10: 1-59716-207-8 (library binding)
  ISBN-13: 978-1-59716-214-2 (pbk.)
  ISBN-10: 1-59716-214-0 (pbk.)
  1. Zombies – Juvenile literature. I. Title.

  GR581.P55 2007
  398'.45 – dc22
                            2006015290

For more information, write to Bearport Publishing Company, Inc., 101 Fifth Avenue, Suite 6R, New York, New York 10003. Printed in the United States of America.

10 9 8 7 6 5 4 3 2

The Tales of Horror series was originally developed by ticktock Media Ltd.

Table of Contents

What Is a Zombie?

Legends and other stories describe zombies as dead people who have been brought back to life. A scratch or bite from one of these **fiends**, however, can turn a living person into a zombie, too.

In movies, zombies stumble around with their eyes staring straight ahead and their mouths wide open. Large groups of these monsters often attack humans, tearing them to pieces. The zombies are looking for their favorite food—human brains!

Although most people don't believe in zombies, these creatures play an important role in several different **cultures**. Read on to experience the chills of each culture's zombie tales. Then decide what you believe.

Voodoo

Zombies first appeared in **voodoo** stories from Haiti, an island nation in the Caribbean. Voodoo is a religion from Africa. Slaves brought the religion to Haiti in the 1700s.

The New Zombie

About 40 years ago, a new kind of zombie began to appear in movies and books. Its rotting body is covered in wriggling **maggots**, and it smells very bad. These new zombies, called **toxic** zombies, come to life when **radiation** or poisonous chemicals leak into burial grounds. These creatures can't feel pain. So, even when a toxic zombie is badly injured, it can still attack.

While zombies can feed during the night or day, toxic zombies prefer to hunt at night. Although they can't move fast, they can smell fresh blood from far away. They can also hear a person's breathing from across the street.

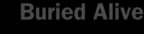

Buried Alive

Long ago, people were sometimes accidentally buried alive. These people were often in a **coma**, which their doctors mistook for death. When thieves dug up their graves to steal jewelry, the corpses seemed to come back to life! This experience may have played a role in the zombie myth.

Voodoo Zombies

Zombies under another person's control are called voodoo zombies. These creatures appear in stories from the Caribbean, Central and South America, and the southern United States.

Voodoo zombies are made when sorcerers, called **houngans**, feed their victims a special powder. As soon as the powder gets into the victim, the person seems to die. While the victim is aware of what is happening, he or she cannot react. In fact, the new zombie has no control over its body at all.

After the victim is buried, the houngan secretly digs the person up and feeds him or her more powder. From that time on, the voodoo zombie is the houngan's very own slave.

Zombie Drugs

The effects of zombie powder are said to last for up to two days. Many of the houngan's powders are made from poisons taken from animals. Poisons from the spiky puffer fish (left), the hyla tree frog, and the cane toad are among those used. Other zombie powders are made from the leaves of the datura tree.

Zombie-Proof

According to zombie movies and books, there are several steps people can take to stay safe when zombies are on the prowl:

- Lock all doors and windows in the house.
- If possible, stay inside and wait for help.
- Have food, water, flashlights, and an emergency radio on hand.
- Use earplugs to block out zombie moans.
- Wear tight clothing so there is nothing for zombies to grab onto.

If zombies do get inside a house, people should slip outside and run. However, they should avoid open areas, such as roads, where one can easily be spotted.

Soul of the Dead

The English word *zombie* has been around for about 200 years. It comes from the African word *nzambi*, which means "the soul of a dead person."

Destroying Zombies

It's not easy to stop a zombie—or so the legends say. Magic potions and spells have no effect on it. The only way to end a zombie's killing spree is to chop off its head with an ax or sword.

People tracking zombies should look for signs of freshly eaten bodies. They should also listen closely for moans. If they can hear any, the zombies can't be very far away. Most important of all: zombie hunters should always work in teams, never alone!

The good news is that zombies don't live forever. They only live as long as it takes for their bodies to rot away.

Hot Zombies

Toxic zombies do not fear fire. When they go up in flames, they don't even notice. They become living torches, setting ablaze everything they touch.

Viking Draugrs

Some stories of zombie-like creatures are many hundreds of years old. One scary legend comes from the **Vikings**.

When the body of a dead warrior was placed in its tomb, the Vikings believed that the body came back to life. These bodies were called draugrs. Some draugrs attacked the living. Others stayed in their tombs, guarding their treasure.

Draugrs had superhuman strength and could only be destroyed by a hero. The hero had to cut off the draugr's head from its body and then leap between the head and body before they hit the ground. Then the draugr's body was burnt and the ashes thrown into the sea.

Magical Draugrs

Draugrs were said to have magical powers. Sometimes they changed into animals such as cats. In some stories, a person killed by a draugr became zombie-like.

Golems

In Jewish folklore, golems are zombie-like creatures. Jewish religious leaders and teachers, called rabbis, created them from clay and mud. Golems were used as servants. They could not speak or disobey their masters.

The golem was brought to life using the **Hebrew** word *emet*, which means "truth." *Emet* was written on the golem's forehead or on a clay tablet put under its tongue.

Sometimes a golem grew too big and hurt people. The rabbi would then turn the golem back into dust by erasing the "e" in *emet*, leaving the word *met*. In Hebrew, *met* means "death."

The Legend of the Golem of Prague

In the 1500s, a rabbi in the city of Prague wanted to defend the Jewish people from attacks. The rabbi created a golem, which started killing people. When the city promised to stop the violence against the Jews, the rabbi turned the golem back into dust.

Revenants

In England, zombies were called revenants during the **Middle Ages**. People back then believed that anyone who had led a wicked life would rise from their grave to haunt the living.

Since revenants were dead bodies, they were blamed for spreading disease. In some countries, people tied up the arms and legs of dead bodies to stop them from becoming revenants. Sometimes the lips were also sewn shut.

Some people believed that a powerful wizard could make a special revenant. The wizard could bring the body of a dead hero to life to carry out a dangerous mission. Although the revenant would be as powerful as the hero was in life, his actions would be under the wizard's control.

Skeleton Zombies

Thousands of years before revenants and draugrs, the Greeks wrote about zombie-like creatures. In the ancient myth of Jason and the Argonauts, Jason and his men battle skeleton warriors. In one version of the story, Jason jumps into the sea. The zombie-like skeletons follow him, but they sink to the bottom!

19

Mummies

Mummies are dead bodies that have been **preserved** and wrapped in cloth. They have been found in China, Japan, Peru, and Egypt. Stories of mummies coming back to life have been told for years.

Many mummy tales may have started with an ancient Egyptian myth. In the myth, the god Osiris is killed by his brother Seth. Osiris's body is cut up and scattered across Egypt. Osiris's wife, Isis, finds all the body parts. When she ties the parts together with cloth, Osiris comes back to life.

How Not to Rot

The ancient Egyptians believed that a person could not pass into the **afterlife** if one's body had rotted. To prevent rotting, workers dried the body with special salts and wrapped it in cloth strips.

Chinese Hopping Corpses

China has its very own zombie, the hopping **corpse**. A touch from one of these monsters will kill a person instantly. Jiangshi, or "stiff corpses," feed on people to take their life force.

Why, however, do the jiangshi hop? When a person dies, **rigor mortis** sets in and muscles stiffen. Since the corpses can't bend their legs, they have to hop to get around.

Hopping corpses are very easy to spot. These zombies usually wear burial clothes from the time of the Chinese Qing rulers (1644–1911). These clothes have been out of fashion for many years.

Sniffing Out Victims

The hopping corpses are blind. The only way they can find victims is by sniffing the air for the scent of human breath. So, if a jiangshi is near, it's a good idea to have some sticky rice on hand. It's one of the few things that will stop them in their tracks!

Ghouls

Zombies in Middle-Eastern folklore are called ghouls. These creatures have very thin faces with bulging yellow eyes. They have long arms and short legs. Ghouls usually live underground in tombs and like to wander around graveyards.

A ghoul has a huge mouth that is lined with rows of tiny, razor-sharp teeth. While toxic zombies only eat living people, a ghoul loves human flesh so much that it also eats dead bodies.

The sun's rays make a ghoul weak, so it only goes looking for meat at night. Luckily for the ghoul, it sees well at night and can smell human flesh from far away.

The Bogeyman

One of the most famous ghouls of all time is the bogeyman. It hides under beds or in closets, waiting for its victim to fall asleep. Then it leaps out of its hiding place. Fortunately, the bogeyman usually only wants to scare its victims—not hurt them.

Frankenstein

The author Mary Shelley created one of the most famous zombie-like monsters of all time in her book *Frankenstein* (1818). In her story, scientist Victor Frankenstein creates a monster in his laboratory by sewing together body parts from dead people. The monster is not a mindless zombie, however. He knows how he was created, and he feels emotions and pain.

Eventually, the monster gets lonely and asks Frankenstein to create a female monster to be his wife. Frankenstein makes the female but then decides it was a mistake and destroys her. The monster becomes so angry that he kills the scientist's wife.

Zombies of the Future

Some people think the story of Frankenstein is a warning: trying to change nature can be dangerous. Today, some people worry that scientists might be able to create mindless monsters by using **genetic engineering**. This process allows scientists to change the nature of living things, such as their size, hair color, and intelligence.

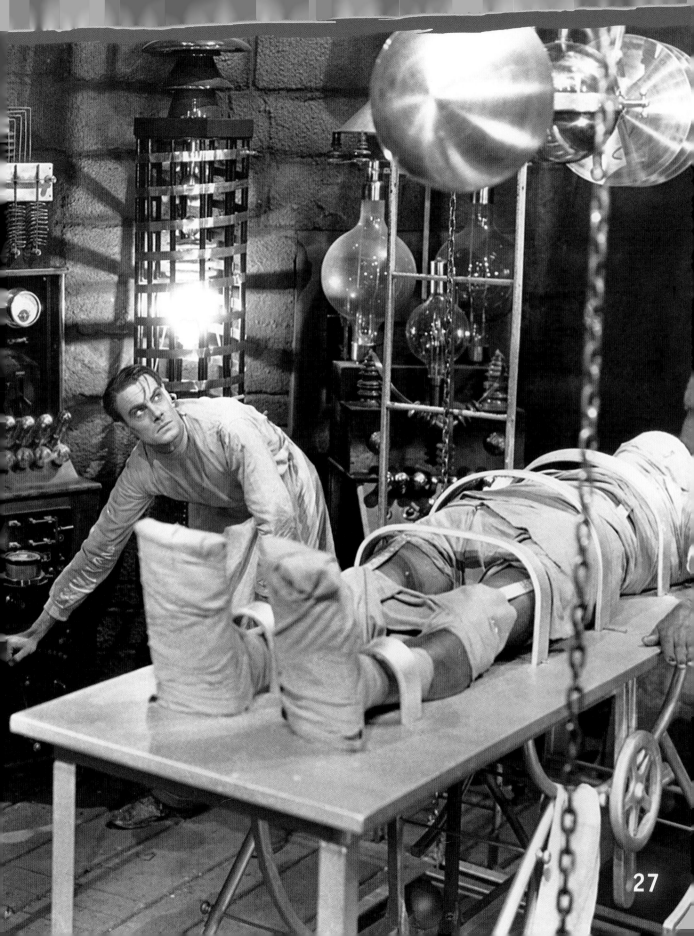

On the Screen

Zombies have been the subject of many scary movies and TV shows. The first movie to use the word "zombie" in its title was *White Zombie* (1932). In this film, a factory owner uses walking corpses as slaves.

Night of the Living Dead (1968) was the first film to show the toxic zombies we know today. The zombies were brought to life by a spacecraft carrying radiation from Venus.

Since *Night of the Living Dead*, toxic zombies have appeared in countless movies, such as *Shaun of the Dead* (2004). Special effects are used to show the rotting bodies and bloody attacks on frightened humans.

Computer Zombies

Many computer games feature zombies as enemies. In the game *Resident Evil,* scientists turn into zombies after a virus escapes from a secret government laboratory. In *Zombies Ate My Neighbors*, the goal is to save your neighbors from hungry zombies.

A scene from the movie
Shaun of the Dead

Do Zombies Exist?

In 1937, crowds in Haiti said they saw a woman named Felicia Felix-Mentor wandering around their village. Yet she had been dead for 30 years! The woman's skin was pale and her eyelashes had fallen out. People said she was a zombie.

In 1980, a man believed to have been dead since 1962 showed up in a Haitian village. Clairvius Narcisse said he'd been given a poison that made him appear dead. After he was buried, he claimed that a sorcerer dug him up and brought him back to life to work as a slave.

Are these zombie sightings the work of overactive imaginations? Or do zombies really exist? While no one knows for certain, thinking about zombies can certainly be good scary fun!

Bug Zombies

The amazing jewel wasp can turn a cockroach into a real-life zombie! First the wasp injects poison into the cockroach's brain. The wasp then grabs the cockroach's feelers to guide it back to the wasp's nest. There, the cockroach is fed to the wasp's young.

31

Glossary

afterlife (AF-tur-*life*) the life a person has after he or she dies

coma (KOH-muh) a state of deep unconsciousness caused by an injury, an illness, or drugs

corpse (KORPS) a dead body

cultures (KUHL-churz) the customs, ideas, art, and traditions that make up people's ways of life

fiends (FEENDZ) evil people or spirits

genetic engineering (juh-NET-ik en-juh-NIHR-ing) when scientists make changes to living things in order to give them certain characteristics

Hebrew (HEE-broo) language of the Jewish people

houngans (hoon-JANS) voodoo priests, usually from Haiti, who can turn people into zombies

legends (LEJ-uhnds) stories that are handed down from the past and are generally believed to be true by those who tell them

maggots (MAG-uhts) flies at the early, worm-like stage of their life cycle

Middle Ages (MID-uhl AJE-iz) a time period in European history from about AD 500 to around 1500

preserved (pri-ZURVD) made to last

radiation (*ray*-dee-AY-shuhn) a kind of powerful energy

rigor mortis (RIG-ur MORT-iss) a condition after death in which the muscles of the body stiffen

toxic (TOK-sik) poisonous

Vikings (VYE-kingz) seafaring warriors from Norway, Denmark, and Sweden who lived from the late 700s to about 1100

voodoo (VOO-doo) a religion in which followers believe that, while in a trance, they can contact their dead ancestors

Index